For Ginger, my most important part

Special thanks to the students of Stacie Nakai's sixth-grade life science
class (Seoul Foreign School, Seoul, Korea), who were the inspiration for this
book. Thanks also to Tim Nolan, A.N.P., and David M. Schuster, M.D., for so
diligently checking my anacomical poems for anatomical correctness.

A. W.

To Greta and Julian
G. C.

Text copyright © 2003 by Allan Wolf
Illustrations copyright © 2003 by Greg Clarke

First edition 2003

Library of Congress Cataloging-in-Publication Data
Wolf, Allan.
The blood-hungry spleen : and other poems about our parts / Allan Wolf ;
illustrated by Greg Clarke. —1st ed.
p.   cm.
Summary: More than thirty poems describe individual parts of the body and
what they do for us, and for some parts, such as the face, the verses
describe how we communicate nonverbally with other people.
ISBN 0-7636-1565-X
1. Body, Human—Juvenile poetry. 2. Body language—Juvenile poetry.
3. Children's poetry, American.
[1. Body, Human—Poetry. 2. Body language—Poetry.
3. American poetry.] I. Clarke, Greg, date, ill. II. Title.
PS3623.O54 O96 2003
811'.54—dc21   2002020711

2 4 6 8 10 9 7 5 3 1

Printed in China

This book was typeset in Triplex Serif Light.
The illustrations were done in acrylic.

Candlewick Press
2067 Massachusetts Avenue
Cambridge, Massachusetts 02140

visit us at www.candlewick.com

The Blood-Hungry Spleen

and Other Poems About Our Parts

Allan Wolf

Allan Wolf

illustrated by Greg Clarke

CANDLEWICK PRESS

CAMBRIDGE, MASSACHUSETTS

Contents

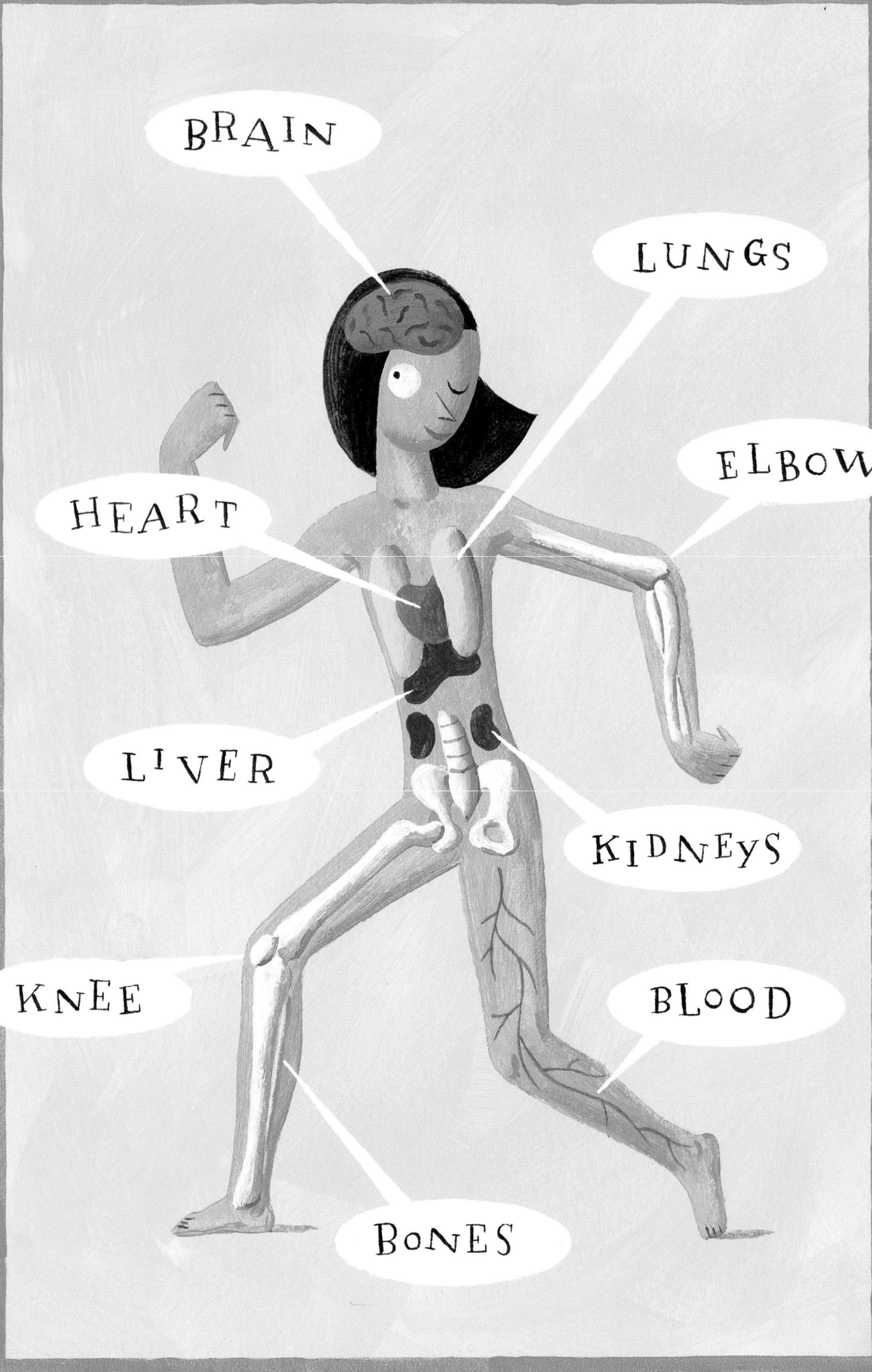

BRAIN

LUNGS

ELBOW

HEART

LIVER

KIDNEYS

KNEE

BLOOD

BONES

Our Amazing Body Language

Our amazing body language!
It's the way the body talks.
Not so much the *words* it uses,
but the way it ticks and tocks.
For its parts all work together
like a tight self-winding clock.
Hooray for our amazing body language!

Sometimes our body talk is loud:
a sneeze, a burp, a cry.
Sometimes our body talk is soft:
a beating heart, a sigh.
Sometimes the talk is soundless as
a silent blinking eye.
Hooray for our amazing body language!

Our body parts are singing out
in choral harmony.
The liver, kidneys, bones, and blood,
the lungs, brain, elbows, knees,
and every other part of us:
a body symphony.
Let's hear it! Our amazing body language!
Let's cheer it! Our amazing body language!
Hip-hip-hooray for our amazing body language!

Skin

It's on your face. Beneath your hair.
It's here. It's there. It's everywhere.
It's on your elbows and your knees.
It covers those. It covers these.
It hangs on tight beneath your shirt.
It's in the dark beneath your skirt.
It heals itself when it gets hurt.
Your skin. Your skin. Your skin.

You've basically two layers of skin.
The outer layer is very thin.
The *epidermis* is its name,
your largest organ, so they claim.
The surface of this layer is dead.
And though you cannot see it shed,
it does, while brand-new cells are fed
from just beneath your skin.

That's where the second layer lies,
the *dermis* and it's just your size.
It senses pressure, pain, and touch.
It sweats when you play ball and such.
It holds the hair tight to your head.
Pierre, Rosita, Franz, or Fred,
each body on the planet's spread
with skin, with skin, with skin.

It covers these. It covers those.
It's on your fingers and your toes.
It's in your ears and up your nose.
Your skin. Your skin. Your skin.
It wraps around your throat and chin.
It keeps germs out. It keeps you in.
The skin that we are *all* born in.
Your skin. Your skin. Your skin.

Face It

Your face is very versatile:
It frowns a frown. It smiles a smile.
It looks ahead. It says, "Good Day."
It stays up front and leads the way.

Your face is almost always showing,
even when it's cold and snowing.
It wears a mask on Halloween,
but mostly it is always seen.

Your face. The place where you display
your happiness and sorrow.
The same face you had yesterday.
The one you'll have tomorrow.

Your Nose Makes Sense

Your nose is a bumper protecting your face
when you walk, by mistake, into doors.
Your nose can allow you to win a close race.
It can wake up the house when it snores.

Your nose is important. It helps you breathe air,
but before the air reaches your lungs,
your nose filters dust with its tiny nose hairs.
If the air's really cold, your nose runs.

It's quite a good smeller, but don't take offense
that a dog's nose can smell even better!
Your *own* nose detects more than 10,000 scents,
and a dog nose is typically wetter.

Open Eyes

We're sphericals.
Twin miracles.
We flutter lids and lashes.
We see the morning.
See it shine!
Squinting.
Sunlight flashes!
Twinkle.
Shimmer.
Glint and blaze.
Lighten.
Brighten.
Blink!
Stare and study.
Watch and gaze.
Wonder.
Wander.
Wink!

See the sun sink out of sight.
Weary.
Drifting.
Weep.
Comes the night.
Turn out the light.
No more gazing.
Now we're glazing.

Dropping,

drooping,

closing,
slowly

sleep.

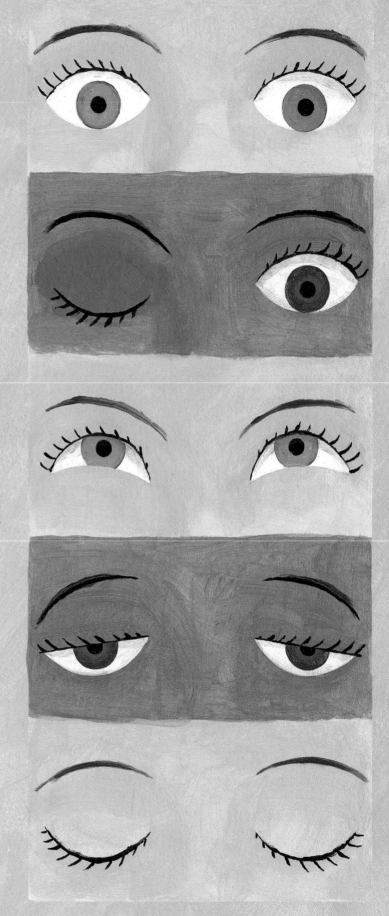

The Ear Poem

Hear ye, hear ye! Listen up!
I have two friends to introduce.
Although they mostly hang around,
I find them both to be of use.

On my left is La-Dee-Dee
and on my right is Siss-Boom-Bah.
And though the two have never met,
two closer friends you never saw.

They work together, La and Siss,
to help me hear whatever is said,
and help me *see* the things I hear
by hooking my glasses to my head.

And though both Siss and La own drums,
politely they don't play them.
I think that I have lovely ears.
I'm happy to display them.

Lip Service

Around your mouth you've got two lips
to help you whistle, smooch, and sip.
They help you say "Birds," "Bugs," and "Bees."
They help you say, "More pancakes, please."

Without your lips, your lonely tongue
could not lick lips when dinner's done.
In place of where your lips had been
you'd have a constant toothy grin.

You couldn't blow a candle out.
You couldn't pucker, purse, or pout.
You couldn't blow a loving kiss.
Or make a silly sound like this:

The Tongue
or Any Muscle This Ugly Has Got to Have Good Taste

And now let me tell you, my friends, of the tongue.
The muscle that does almost all of the talking.
It's in every mouth, narrow, wide, old, and young.
Without it, our singing would sound more like squawking.

Your tongue is for chewing. For curling. For clicking.
It fits in your mouth like a bug in a rug.
Your tongue is for tasting and lollipop licking.
But hey, folks, let's face it. It looks like a slug!

One Tooth, Two Tooth, White Tooth, Looth Tooth

One tooth. Two teeth.
Baby chew teeth.
Twenty bright teeth.
Pearly white teeth.
Daily use teeth.
Wiggle loose teeth.
Three teeth. Four teeth.
In grow more teeth.
Grown-up new teeth.
Thirty-two teeth.
Not quite right teeth.

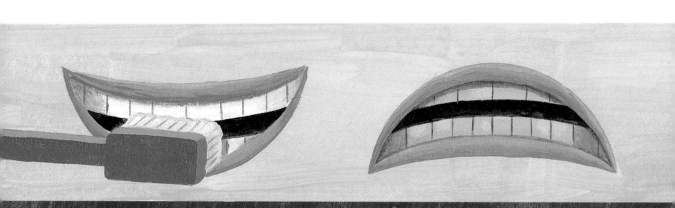

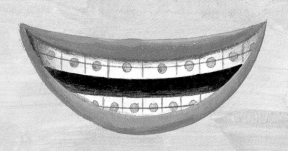

Overbite teeth.
Five teeth. Six teeth.
Gotta fix teeth.
Seven teeth. Eight teeth.
Now they're straight teeth.
Nine teeth. Ten teeth.
Brush and tend teeth.
Up teeth. Down teeth.
Smile teeth. Frown teeth.
Too much cake teeth.
Ouch! Toothache teeth.
Treat them well or you'll have fake teeth!

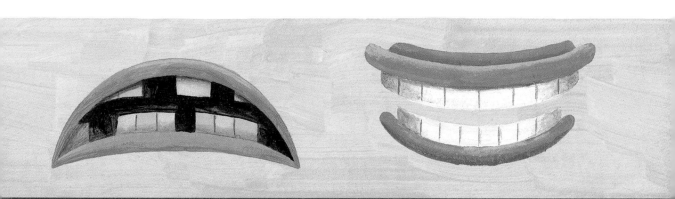

Ode to My Fingers

You wave and tickle, tap and hold.
You help me tie my shoestrings.
You whistle, wiggle, flap, and fold,
wear ball gloves, and display my rings.
And I know, no matter what I do,
I can always count on you.

You stand up straight to show I'm right.
You loosen stuck-shut pickle jars.
You're with me each and every night
to track the paths of falling stars.
And even in some foreign land,
I know you'll always be on hand.

You're always ready with a nail
upon your fingertips.
You're always ready without fail
ensuring that my zipper zips.
And if I feel a need to pick my nose,
you tend to be a better fit than toes.

Ode to My Toes

Thank you, toes, for all you do.
You always understand me.
I dedicate this poem to you
because I think you're dandy.

It must be just unbearable
to spend all day cramped in a shoe
and hurt your feelings terrible
when everyone looks down on you.

Those times you feel a little low
just think of all your talents:
like dangling in water and walking tiptoe
and helping the feet keep their balance.

The toes are who the fingers call
when doing math gets out of hand.
And who in this world is a match for you all
when it comes down to wiggling in sand?

Thirteen Ways of Looking at Your Knees and Elbows

I
The elbow is the joint
where the bone of the
upper arm (*humerus*)
meets the two bones of the
lower arm (*radius* and *ulna*).

II
The knee is the joint
where the bone of the
upper leg (*femur*)
meets the two bones of the
lower leg (*tibia* and *fibula*).

III
Your left elbow is in love
with your right elbow, only
the right elbow doesn't know.

IV
The knee wears a cap
all year long,
even in church.

V
If elbows did not bend
you could not scratch
your nose.

VI
If knees did not bend
there would be no
marriage proposals.

VII
Elbows and hair bows
do not look alike.

VIII
When two knees meet
they say, "I love you.
I want you. I kneed you."

IX
Elbows like to link
on a long lazy walk.

X
When knees watch
scary movies they
kn-kn-knock.

XI
A knee is still a knee,
and an elbow is still an elbow,
even when they are not bent.

XII
Knees and elbows
gather together to think
and to watch sporting events.

XIII
Elbows and knees
are bends in the road
of your body.

You Cannot Rankle
the Sturdy Ankle

Your sturdy ankle, strong and straight,
its whole life it does dedicate
to holding up your body's weight
to keep you standing tall.

Your ankle features swivel action!
Shock-absorbing track star traction!
Guaranteed foot satisfaction.
Yes! And that's not all!

Your sturdy ankle does its share,
for if your ankle wasn't there
your foot would fly into the air
each time you'd kick a ball!

Bone Chart

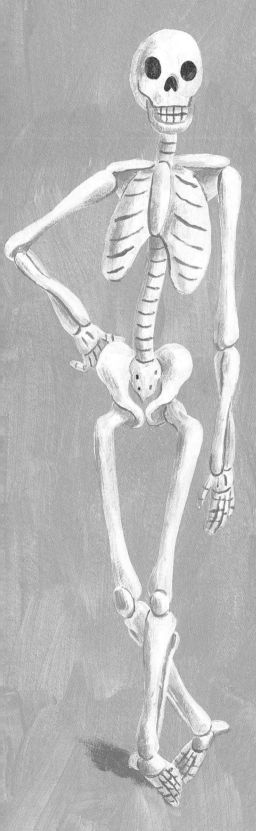

Your bones hold you up like the frame of a house.
Be you boy. Be you girl. Be you lion or mouse.

Your skull is a bone that encloses your brain.
It holds up your hat, and it keeps out the rain.

Just under your skull is the trusty jawbone.
It helps you to chew and to talk on the phone.

Your neck bones and back bones are called *vertebrae*.
They help keep your spinal cord out of harm's way.

The collarbone works with its friend, shoulder blade.
Because of their union a shoulder is made.

The arm bones come next, followed close by the hands.
They help you give hugs and direct marching bands.

The ribs are a wonder; in all there's twelve pair
protecting your lungs as they help you breathe air.

The hipbone, or pelvis, is next with a flair.
It helps you to hula and sit in a chair.

For strength, your eight leg bones are second to none.
They help you to hop and allow you to run.

All told, you have just over two hundred bones.
Two hundred and six, if you really must know.
There's fifty-two bones in your two feet alone!
And that is your bone chart, from head bone to toe.

Boneless

A boneless boy would be a bore,
his body in a muddle.
He'd lie in silence on the floor.
He'd be a human puddle.

And if my poodle had no bones,
she'd be no fun to cuddle.
And even when she was full-grown,
she'd be a poodle puddle.

We all need bones to give us shape,
from little boys to poodles.
That's why our limbs are strong and straight
instead of limp, like noodles.

WITHOUT BONES

WITH BONES

Your Navel Is No Mystery

Your bellybutton is a mark
that tells you how you got your start.
For in the womb, long time ago,
you couldn't eat or drink, and so
your mother was attached to you,
about midbelly, by a tube.
Umbilical's its proper name,
and where they snipped it off became
your bellybutton, round and playful
(in fancy talk it's called the *navel*).
And that's the truth, and so you see
your navel is no mystery:
It marks the spot your family
attached you to the family tree
when you began to be.

A Sad Tale
or Hey, Who Stole My Seat?

"Find your seats quickly," the bus driver yawned.
So I looked for mine quickly, but found it was gone!
"Oh, bus driver! Help!" I cried. "Something's amiss."
He answered, "I'll get to the bottom of this!"
In vain, we searched everywhere, hoping to find
some clue to the thief who had pinched my behind.
Weeks later, I don't know *who* stole my rear end.
And though it sounds cheeky, I've lost my best friend.
Without my behind, I am in quite a muddle.
I'll have to have surgeons perform a re-buttal!
But meanwhile if, someday, you happen to meet
the bandit who's sitting on my stolen seat,
be rude to him, glare at him, tweak him and twank him!
Stomp his toe! Call the police!

. . . Just don't spank him.

You Can't Beat Your Heart

And now your most important part:
the tireless, pulsing, pumping heart!
Lub-dubb, lub-dubb, lub-dubb—it goes.
You run, it speeds. You stop, it slows.

It squeezes tight and then lets go,
which causes circulation flow.
Lub-dubb, lub-dubb—without delay.
One hundred thousand times a day.

No matter what you do or say.
A kid. A man. A newborn babe.
Lub-dubb, lub-dubb—it keeps the beat.
When you're awake. When you're asleep.

It sends the blue blood to the lungs.
It sends the red blood to the cells.
Lub-dubb, lub-dubb—you've got just one.
So love your heart and treat it well.

Lub-dubb, lub-dubb—your heartbeat hums.
Lub-dubb, lub-dubb, lub-dubb—it thrums.
Lub-dubb, lub-dubb—a rum tum-tum.
Your heart's a blood and muscle drum!

Lub-dubb lub-dubb lub-dubb lub-dubb lub-dubb

lub-dubb lub-dubb lub-dubb lub-dubb lub-dubb lu-dubb

A Superior Vena Cava B Aorta
C Pulmonary Aorta D Rt. Atrium E Lt. Atrium
F Right Ventricle G Left Ventricle

Shy Silent Rivers

They start at the heart.
The heart's where they end.
Shy silent rivers flow under your skin.

Arteries rush the blood away
to hungry cells in every part.
Every port. Distant limbs.
Tributaries. Tiny slivers.
Oxygen, food, and life to deliver.
Shy red silent rivers.

Veins return the blood on home.
Weary blood cells. Used and blue.
Replenished in your heart lung nest.
Never rest. Never rest.
Ever turning. Tireless givers.
Shy blue silent rivers.

Rejuvenation. Silent rivers.
Intestine, stomach, lungs, and liver.
Circulation. Blue red rivers.
Whisper forward.
Life deliver.
Tireless shy
silent
rivers.

The Blood-Hungry Spleen

To the left of your stomach, a deep violet-red,
a filter's at work filling blood cells with dread:
The red blood cell graveyard! It's not Halloween.
I'm talking about that blood basher, the *spleen*.

It's the blood-hungry spleen. Blood cells better beware.
Just enter in here and you exit out there.
But *not* if you're sickly. Gasp! What's that I hear?
It's the sound of sick blood cells all screaming in fear!

It's five inches long, and it's three inches wide.
If you're an old blood cell, you best run and hide.
And if you're a tired blood cell, you best stay in bed.
It's the blood-hungry spleen, and it wants to be fed!

Lungs

Your lungs are like two pink balloons.
Take a breath and shout!
They grow big when the air goes in.
They shrink when air goes out.

Your lungs are like two pink balloons.
Take a breath and sigh.
Without your lungs you couldn't find
the breath to help you cry.

Your lungs are like two pink balloons.
Breathe, then sneeze. Ah-choo!
Your lungs can fill with liquid
when you've got a touch of flu.

Your lungs are like two pink balloons.
Exhale now, then yawn!
Your lungs remind you when you're tired
and all your pep is gone.

Your lungs are like two pink balloons.
Blow the candles out!
Your birthday wouldn't be the same
without your lungs about.

Inhale! Exhale! Inhale! Exhale!
In! Out! In!
How many times can you say your own name
before you must stop to breathe in?

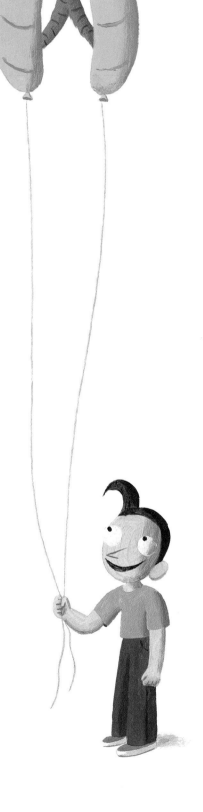

Your Muscles Keep You Moving

Involuntary muscles,
like your stomach and your heart,
are always working overtime
to give you a head start.

They never stop. They never rest.
They live one step ahead.
They're even working for you
when you're fast asleep in bed.

But *voluntary* muscles,
like your legs and arms and hands,
rely upon their boss (the brain)
to relay its commands.

The muscles that you use to breathe
are just a bit contrary:
*in*voluntary mostly;
but they *can* be voluntary.

And so, too, are your eyelids;
automatically they blink.
But you *can* take control of them.
To test this out, just wink.

Your Brain's the Boss

Your brain's the boss, though truth be told,
your brain's no beauty to behold.
It looks just like a Jell-O mold,
but, oh, it's marvelous!

Laugh and talk and yell and cry.
Fume and fret and sing and sigh.
Whistle, walk, and wave goodbye.
Your brain is a great inspiration.

Muscles and movement and coordination.
Learning, intelligence, imagination.
Heartbeat, digestion, emotion, sensation.
Your brain is a thing to behold!

Though, truth be told,
it *still* looks like a Jell-O mold.

This Poem Has Been Brought to You by Your Five Senses

Warm pajamas, burps, kazoos,
stars, hot chocolate, *I love you*'s,
perfume, popcorn, comfy shoes,
a hundred different blues.

Fresh-mown grass, hugs, puppy fur,
flowers, sunsets, kitten purrs,
after-bedtime whispered words,
wobbly newborn birds.

The Story of Ow!

The toe hollered, "Ow!" to the nerve.
The "Ow!" echoed onward up the spine.
As the "Ow!" sped its way along the spinal cord,
the "Ow!" set a world-record time.

When the "Ow!" made its way to the brain,
the brain thought, "Ow! That's a pain."
So the brain sent the "Ow!" to the vocal cords,
which said,

"Excuse me please, but you're standing on my foot!"

Spit

Saliva, better known as spit;
it seems our mouths are full of it.
To see your spit at work, don't spew it;
bite a bit of bread and chew it.
Your *salivary glands* produce
saliva, a digestive juice
that helps to turn the bread to mush,
assisting the *esophagus*
(a muscular and lengthy tube)
in swallowing the food you've chewed.
Although some folks think spit is rude,
your spit helps you digest your food.

Your Stomach, the Belly-Brewing Wonder

Your stomach is a dancer!
It moves its muscled walls
to dance alone long after
you have left the banquet halls.

Your stomach is a brewer!
Its job is to produce
a secret mix ingredient
that's known as *gastric juice*.

Your stomach is a blender!
It's mixing all the time,
churning up your food
into a mixture known as *chyme*.

Your stomach is a worker!
Its strong walls work all day
to blend the gastric juice and food
and send it on its way.

Your stomach is a dancer
and a brewer and a blender.
A worker and a muscler
and a squeezer and a tumbler.
A mixer and a masher
and a mover and a rumbler.
A churner. A burner.
A turner. A thunder.

Your stomach is a belly-brewing wonder!

MR. TUMMY'S GASTRIC JUICE
DIGESTIVE AID

Kidney Trouble
(Poem for Two Voices)

I'm Kenneth.

	I'm Kendra.
And we are your kidneys.	And we are your kidneys.
I'm the left	
	I'm the right
and we make quite a pair.	and we make quite a pair.

42

We're leaders!

We're *filters*.
We filter the blood

and remove the impurities

take out the garbage that's
hiding in there.

hiding in there.

As the blood travels through us
we pluck out the poisons!

Kind of like gardeners
pulling up weeds.

We flush out the waste
in a liquid called urine.

But most of us just call it pee.

This urine—

this *pee*, it is passed down a tube

called the *ureter*

into a bag

called the *bladder*.

Who cares what you call it?

I do!

What's it matter?

You're making me mad!

Well you're making me madder!

I'm Kenneth.

I'm Kendra.
And we are your kidneys.

And we are your kidneys.
I'm the left

I'm the right
and on *that* we agree.

and on *that* we agree.
We're leaders!

We're *filters*.

We generate urine!

He means to say
we make the pee.

we make the pee.

Moving the Food Along

The small intestine (narrow, coiled)
absorbs the food you eat
by breaking into molecules
your vegetables and meat
and bread and milk, each curly fry
and after-dinner treat.
Your small intestine zigs and zags
for twenty winding feet.
Your small intestine moves the food along.

The large intestine (wide and scrunched)
is shorter, just five feet.
So Large picks up where Small left off
and doesn't miss a beat.
It takes out water, making poop,
and so its job's complete.
Your large intestine moves the food along.

Your rectum is a smaller tube,
a mere six inches long.
Your rectum is the final one to move the food along.

Consider the Anus

The anus is the exit
for the waste your body makes,
a thankless job
(but *someone* has to do it).
Your anus is reliable
and rarely makes mistakes.
It loves its job
(though most of us poo-poo it).

Your Hormones Are Exciting

Your hormones are exciting!
They stir your body up.
They're made by glands (called *endocrine*)
and give your body pluck.
Your hormones are the messengers
who trickle from the glands,
and, following the blood stream,
carry chemical commands
to tissues and to organs,
head-to-toe and hand-to-hand.
Without your hormones, life is like
a dance without a band.

You jump when some mean kid says, "Boo!"
It's all stirred up by hormones.
You flinch although you try not to.
It's all because of hormones.
One day you're short. And then you're tall.
Your favorite shoes are way too tight.
Your favorite pants are way too small.
Your bike won't even fit you right.
Your world is slowly shrinking
while the rest of you expands.
Without your hormones, life is like
a dance without a band.

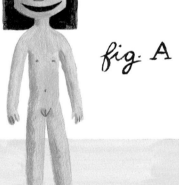

fig. A

A change called *puberty*'s begun.
It's all stirred up by hormones.
You've grown some hair where there was none.
It's all because of hormones.
If you're a girl your hips get wide.
If you're a boy your voice gets deep.
You feel all turned around inside.
One day you laugh. One day you weep.
Thus hormones make you who you are,
and who you are is grand.
Without your hormones, life is like
a dance without a band.

fig. B

Boy Parts

Between his belly and his knees,
each boy and man has one of these.
The *penis* is its proper name,
a treasure only boys can claim.

This is the place from which boys pee.
And also (after puberty)
the penis makes itself of use
when dads and mommies reproduce.

And dangling between his legs
beneath the penis, slightly back,
two balls the shape of robins' eggs
are held within the *scrotum* sack.

These *testicles* are dear indeed
because they make the sperm dads need
to fertilize a mother's egg,
which grows into a you or me.

Girl Parts

Between their bellies and their knees,
girls and women all have these.
Vagina is its proper name,
a treasure only girls can claim.

An opening between girls' legs,
protected by soft folds of skin,
it opens on a passageway,
which leads up to the *womb* within.

All females have a special room
inside their tummies, called a womb.
It's called the *uterus* as well.
It's strong and stretchy and can swell

to many times its normal girth
as baby grows before its birth.
Nearby the womb are two round shapes
about the size of two large grapes.

These *ovaries* are dear indeed
because they hold the eggs moms need
to join together with dad's sperm
and grow into a you or me.

The Cells That Make Us You and Me

They're microscopic miracles.
They're building blocks of life,
the key to every living human being.
Each part of you is made of cells,
each inside part and out,
although your cells are too small to be seen.

But if you use a microscope
to view a cell up close,
you'll see the main parts of the cell (there's three).
The *plasma membrane* is the skin
around the *cytoplasm,*
around a tiny cytoplasm sea.

The moon that sails upon this sea,
the *nucleus,* contains
the DNA that makes us you and me.
The nucleus, the membrane, and
the cytoplasm sea;
without your cells, you simply wouldn't be.

Notes

BRAIN   All right, I may be stretching the truth a tiny bit when I say that your brain controls heartbeat and digestion. Digestion takes place mostly due to automatic chemical reactions. And your heartbeat is automatic too. But your digestion and heart rate can be influenced by your emotions. And emotions live in your brain. For example, if you are nervous about a big soccer game, your heart rate may increase, while your stomach and intestines may stop digesting your food efficiently.

CELLS   Maybe the most amazing body part of all, the cell is the building block that makes up all other body parts. In fact, your body is made up of more than ten trillion (10,000,000,000,000) cells! Every type of cell has its own unique look, but most cells have some sort of *membrane* to enclose the cell's liquid *cytoplasm.* And immersed within this cytoplasm is the cell's *nucleus.*

But cells are more than just a membrane, cytoplasm, and nucleus. The cytoplasm is the home of many other cellular structures, called *organelles,* all with special jobs to do.

EARS   Your ears don't have actual drums like the kind you might beat in a rock 'n' roll band. Deep inside the opening of each ear is a thin membrane called the *eardrum,* because it looks and functions much like the head of a real drum. Sound waves hitting against the eardrum create vibrations that are sent to your brain. That's pretty much how you hear any kind of noise, from a dog barking, to a bat hitting a ball, to the echo of your footsteps in the hall.

HEART   How do I *know* the heart beats one hundred thousand times a day? That's easy. I just did some math. I found out that the average heart beats about 70 beats each minute. Since there are 60 minutes in an hour, I know the heart beats about 60 × 70, or 4,200, times in one hour. There are 24 hours in a day, so I multiplied 4,200 × 24 to get a total of 100,800 "lub-dubbs." I rounded the number down to an even 100,000 because it sounded better in the poem.

Heart rates differ from person to person. Babies' hearts beat about 120 times a minute. Kids' hearts are slower, about 90 beats. The average adult heartbeat can be anywhere from 60 to 100 beats per minute. And athletes who are in tiptop shape may have a heartbeat as low as 40 beats per minute!

SPLEEN   Actually your spleen is not as scary as I've made it sound. But still, this spongy purple fellow works hard. It does a lot more than ridding the body of sick and old blood cells. Like the liver and the kidneys, your spleen is a filter that removes parasites, bacteria, and other assorted junk. Your spleen helps to strengthen your immune system as well because it provides a home for clumps of white blood cells, which release special proteins that kill viruses and other infection-causing organisms.

STOMACH   In the poem "Your Muscles Keep You Moving," I call the stomach a muscle. Not exactly true. This j-shaped bag of an organ is not a muscle. It is, however, covered with layers of muscle that automatically go to work whenever you eat something—say, a cheeseburger.

VOLUNTARY AND INVOLUNTARY MUSCLES   Okay. Okay. Okay. The muscles in your eyelids are not exactly involuntary muscles. Usually your eyelids have to get a direct command from your brain before they open, close, wink, or flutter.

The muscles in your intestines are made of true involuntary muscle, which is why you can keep playing the guitar as your body automatically digests the pepperoni pizza you just ate.

And since we're being so nitpicky about terminology here, the involuntary muscle of the heart is really in a class by itself—called *cardiac muscle*. Cardiac muscle will go on beating even if the brain has stopped bossing the rest of your body around. In fact, if it were removed from your body altogether, your heart muscle would continue to beat—for a while—ALL BY ITSELF! Creepy, yet amazing.

Further Reading

for kids, parents, teachers, librarians, and other amateur anatomists

Anderson, Karen C., and Stephen Cumbaa. *The Bones & Skeleton Game Book: A Challenging Collection of Puzzles and Projects.* New York: Workman, 1993. Covers other body systems in addition to the skeletal system.

Avison, Brigid. *I Wonder Why I Blink and Other Questions About My Body.* New York: Kingfisher Books, 1993.

Balkwill, Frances R. *Cells Are Us.* Minneapolis, Minn.: Carolrhoda Books, 1993.

Harris, Robie H. *It's Perfectly Normal: A Book about Changing Bodies, Growing Up, Sex, and Sexual Health.* Cambridge, Mass.: Candlewick Press, 1994.

———. *It's So Amazing!: A Book about Eggs, Sperm, Birth, Babies, and Families.* Cambridge, Mass.: Candlewick Press, 1999.

Llewellyn, Claire. *The Big Book of Bones: An Introduction to Skeletons.* New York: Peter Bedrick Books, 2001.

Martin, Paul D. *Messengers to the Brain: Our Fantastic Five Senses.* Washington, D.C.: National Geographic Society, 1984.

Parker, Steve. *Brain Surgery for Beginners and Other Major Operations for Minors.* Brookfield, Conn.: Millbrook Press, 1995.

Rowan, Dr. Pete. *Some Body!* New York: Alfred A. Knopf, 1995.

Silverstein, Dr. Alvin, Virginia Silverstein, and Robert Silverstein. Human Body Systems series. New York: Twenty-First Century Books. See individual volumes: *The Digestive System (1995), The Skeletal System (1995), The Muscular System (1995), The Excretory System (1997),* and *The Circulatory System (1997).*

VanCleave, Janice. *The Human Body for Every Kid: Easy Activities That Make Learning Science Fun.* New York: John Wiley & Sons, 1995.

for the serious anatomist

Clemente, Carmine D. *Anatomy: A Regional Atlas of the Human Body.* 4th edition. Philadelphia: Lippincott, Williams & Wilkins, 1997.

Gray, Henry. *Anatomy, Descriptive and Surgical.* Philadelphia: Courage Books, 1999.

O'Toole, Marie T., main editor. *Miller-Keane Encyclopedia and Dictionary of Medicine, Nursing, and Allied Health.* 6th edition. Philadelphia: W. B. Saunders Company, 1997.